DOMINOES

D0602810

The Selfish Giant

QUICK STARTER   250 HEADWORDS

OXFORD
UNIVERSITY PRESS

Great Clarendon Street, Oxford, OX2 6DP, United Kingdom

Oxford University Press is a department of the University of Oxford.
It furthers the University's objective of excellence in research, scholarship,
and education by publishing worldwide. Oxford is a registered trade
mark of Oxford University Press in the UK and in certain other countries

This edition © Oxford University Press 2012

The moral rights of the author have been asserted

First published in Dominoes 2012

2016

10 9 8

ISBN: 978 0 19 424931 7   Book
ISBN: 978 0 19 463905 7   Book and Audio Pack

Printed in China

This book is printed on paper from certified and well-managed sources

ACKNOWLEDGEMENTS

Cover artwork and illustrations by: Scott Altmann

DOMINOES

Series Editors: Bill Bowler and Sue Parminter

The Selfish Giant

Oscar Wilde

Text adaptation by Bill Bowler

Illustrated by Scott Altmann

Oscar Wilde was born in Dublin, Ireland in 1854, and studied Greek and Latin at university in Dublin and Oxford. He wrote short stories for adults, fairy tales for children, and a novel, *The Picture of Dorian Gray* (1891). He also wrote popular comedies for the theatre, including *The Importance of Being Earnest* (1895). He is famous too for his clever and funny sayings. He died in Paris in 1900 at the age of forty-six. *Lord Arthur Savile's Crime and Other Stories* and *The Happy Prince* by Oscar Wilde are also available as Dominoes.

OXFORD
UNIVERSITY PRESS

Story Characters

The Selfish Giant

The little boy

The children

The Snow

The Frost

The North Wind

The Hail

Autumn

Contents

BEFORE READING

This story is about a selfish Giant. What do you think happens in it? Tick the boxes.

a At first, the Giant is … when children play in his garden.

  1 happy

  2 angry

  3 afraid

b The Giant puts … around his garden.

  1 a wall

  2 some shops

  3 a road

c After this, it is always … in the Giant's garden.

  1 autumn

  2 spring

  3 winter

 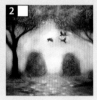

d Later, the Giant makes friends with … .

  1 a little boy

  2 two more giants

  3 a gardener

e In the end, the Giant likes seeing the … in his garden.

  1 birds

  2 children

  3 cats

CHAPTER 1
The Giant comes home

Every afternoon, when **school** finishes, the children play in the **Giant's** garden.

It's a wonderful, big, green garden. There are beautiful flowers in it, and twelve tall trees. **Birds** like sitting and singing in these trees. The children often stop playing and listen to them. 'We're very happy here,' they say.

For seven years, the Giant stays away in Cornwall, at the house of his friend the Cornish Giant. Then, one day, he comes home, and he finds all the children in the garden.

'What are you doing here?' he cries angrily, and the children run away.

school students learn here

giant a very big, tall man or woman

bird an animal that can fly through the sky

'It's my garden,' the Giant says. 'People must understand! And nobody can play here – only me!'

So he puts a **wall around** the garden, with a big **notice** on it.

He is a very **selfish** Giant.

Where can the children go now? They don't like playing in the road. So after school, they walk around the wall and they look at it. And they remember the beautiful garden behind it, too.

READING CHECK

Are these sentences true or false? Tick the boxes.

		True	False
a	The children play in the Giant's garden before school.	☐	☑
b	They are very happy there.	☐	☐
c	The Giant comes home from Cornwall after seven weeks.	☐	☐
d	When he comes back, he's happy to see the children.	☐	☐
e	The children run to the Giant when he arrives.	☐	☐
f	The Giant puts a wall around his garden.	☐	☐
g	He puts a notice on the wall.	☐	☐
h	The children like playing in the road.	☐	☐
i	They forget the Giant's beautiful garden.	☐	☐

GUESS WHAT

What does the Giant do in the next chapter? Tick one box.

a He asks the Cornish Giant to his house. ☐

b He finds a little boy in his house. ☐

c He watches his garden for weeks, but it doesn't change. ☐

d He puts a door in his garden wall. ☐

CHAPTER 2
Always winter

Then the **spring** comes. All over the country there are spring flowers and little birds in the green trees. But in the Selfish Giant's garden it stays **winter**. The birds don't want to sing in it, because there are no children. The trees there stay dark. One beautiful flower puts its head up out of the **ground**. But it sees the notice, and is very sorry for the children. So it goes back under the ground and sleeps again.

Nobody is happy about this – only the **Snow** and the **Frost**. 'Spring doesn't come to this garden!' they cry. 'So we can live here all year! Ha! Ha!'

spring the three months of the year when it is warm, but not hot

winter the coldest three months of the year

ground we walk on this

snow something soft, cold, and white

frost this icy water often covers things thinly at night when it is cold

The Snow puts her cold, white coat on the ground, and the Frost puts **silver** on the dark trees.

They tell the North **Wind**, 'You must stay with us!' So he comes in his big, brown coat. He makes lots of noise up and down the garden, and he moves things here and there all day.

'This is wonderful!' he cries. 'Let's ask the **Hail** here, too!'

So the Hail comes. Every day he sits on the **roof** of the Giant's big, old house. He never stops hitting it noisily, hour after hour. His suit is the colour of smoke. And cold smoke comes from his mouth when he opens it.

silver something that is the colour of an expensive white metal

wind air that moves

hail cold, hard rain

roof the thing on top of a building that stops the rain coming in

The Selfish Giant sits at his window. He looks out at his cold, white garden.

'I don't understand,' he says. 'The spring's very late this year. When is it coming? And when is this winter finishing?'

ACTIVITIES

READING CHECK

Match the characters from Chapter 2 with the sentences.

the Flower

the Frost

the Selfish Giant

the Hail

the North Wind

the Snow

a In . . . . the Selfish Giant . . . . 's garden, it stays winter.

b . . . . puts its head out of the ground.

c . . . . sees . . . . 's notice

and goes under the ground again.

d . . . . puts her cold, white coat on the ground.

e . . . . puts silver on the dark trees.

f . . . . has a big, brown coat.

g . . . . moves things here and there in the garden.

h . . . . sits on the Selfish Giant's roof and hits it noisily.

i . . . . 's suit is the colour of smoke.

j . . . . sits at his window and looks at the garden.

GUESS WHAT

What happens in the next chapter? Tick two sentences.

a ☐ Some cats come to the Selfish Giant's garden.

b ☐ The children come back into the Giant's garden.

c ☐ All the trees in the Selfish Giant's garden die.

d ☐ The winter goes from the Giant's garden.

e ☐ A big cat kills all the birds in the Giant's garden.

f ☐ The Selfish Giant sleeps for a hundred years.

CHAPTER 3
The hole in the wall

The spring and the **summer** never come to the Giant's garden. The **Autumn** brings **golden** apples to most people's gardens, but to the Giant's garden she brings nothing. 'I don't give to selfish people,' she says.

So it is always winter there. And the North Wind, the Hail, the Frost and the Snow run about in it.

One morning, when the Giant opens his eyes in bed, he hears some **music**.

'That's beautiful!' he cries. 'But what is it?' A little bird is singing near his window – that's all. But after the long winter in his garden, the Giant can't remember the noise very well.

summer the hottest three months of the year

autumn the three months of the year between summer and winter

golden the colour of an expensive yellow metal

music people listen or dance to this

Then the Hail stops hitting the roof, and the North Wind is quiet. Suddenly a wonderful **perfume** comes to the Giant through the open window. 'The spring's here at last, I think!' he cries. Then he gets up and looks out.

What a wonderful thing! The children are coming into the garden through a little **hole** in the wall, and they are sitting in the trees. And the trees are happy because the children are back. They begin to **blossom** and move their arms about.

perfume a nice smell

hole an opening in something that you can go through

blossom to have flowers (of a tree); a flower on a tree

The birds are singing happily in the sky. The flowers are coming out of the ground and laughing.

But far across the garden – in one **corner** – it isn't spring. A young boy is standing there. There is frost and snow on his tree, and he cannot get up into it. So he is crying.

corner where the two sides of something meet

READING CHECK

Choose the correct words to complete the sentences.

a The autumn brings *golden* / *red* apples to most gardens.

b She brings *nothing* / *something* to the Giant's garden.

c One day, a *child* / *bird* sings in the Giant's garden.

d Suddenly, the Hail and North Wind make *lots of* / *no* noise.

e A nice *perfume* / *noise* comes through the Giant's window.

f Children go and sit *in* / *under* the Giant's trees.

g Winter leaves *most* / *all* of the Giant's garden.

h A young *girl* / *boy* cries in one corner of the garden.

GUESS WHAT

What happens in the next chapter? Tick the boxes.

	Yes	No
a A tree in the corner of the garden wants to help the little boy.	☐	☐
b The Giant goes out into his garden.	☐	☐
c The children are happy to see the Giant.	☐	☐
d Most of the children run to the Giant.	☐	☐
e The little boy has his head in his hands.	☐	☐
f He looks up, sees the Giant, and cries.	☐	☐
g The Giant puts the little boy up into the tree.	☐	☐
h The children bring back spring to the garden.	☐	☐
i The Giant takes away the garden wall.	☐	☐

CHAPTER 4

The boy in the tree

'Get up, little boy!' says the tree in that corner of the garden, and it puts its **branches** nearer the ground for the young boy. But he is very little, and he can't get on them.

The Giant watches from his window, and his cold **heart** is suddenly warmer.

'Now I see!' he cries. 'The spring doesn't come here because I'm selfish.' He is truly sorry.

'I know!' he says. 'I can put the little boy up in the tree and **knock down** the wall. Then the children can always play in my garden.'

branch part of a tree

heart the centre of feeling in someone

knock down to hit something and break it into pieces

So he goes quietly down to his front door, and he opens it. Then he goes out into the garden.

When the children see him, they are very afraid. So they all run away, and it is winter in the garden again.

But the little boy has his head in his hands. He can't see the Giant. So the Giant goes very quietly over to him. He takes the little boy carefully in his hand, and he puts him up in the tree.

At once, the tree blossoms, and the birds come and sing in it. Then the little boy puts his arms around the Giant's **neck**, and he **kisses** him.

When the **other** children see this, they understand: the Giant isn't bad any more! So they run back into the garden, and the spring comes with them.

'It's your garden now, little children,' the Giant says. Then he takes a big **axe**, and he knocks down the wall.

neck this is between your head and your body

kiss to touch lovingly with your mouth

other different

axe you use this to cut wood

READING CHECK

Correct nine more mistakes in the story.

The tree in the corner of the garden puts its ~~apples~~ ...*branches*... near the ground for the young boy. But the boy is tired, and he can't get on them. The Giant sees this, and his heart is suddenly colder. He goes quietly out of his back door and out into the garden.

The children are happy, and they all run away. But the boy in the corner has his head in his books. He can't see the Giant.

So the Giant puts him up in the tree. Then the boy kills the Giant. After that, all the children walk back into the garden, and winter comes with them.

In the end, the Giant knocks down the wall around the garden with his feet.

GUESS WHAT

What happens in the next chapter? Tick one box for a, b, and c.

a The Giant…
  1 ☐ soon forgets the little boy in the tree.
  2 ☐ plays with the children for many years.
  3 ☐ doesn't like the children's games when he is older.

b The little boy in the tree…
  1 ☐ doesn't come to the Giant's garden for many years.
  2 ☐ visits the Giant again when he is a young man.
  3 ☐ goes and lives in the Giant's house with him.

c The children…
  1 ☐ play in the Giant's garden every afternoon.
  2 ☐ tell the Giant all about the little boy.
  3 ☐ take the Giant to the little boy's home in the town.

CHAPTER 5
The most beautiful flowers

At twelve o'clock that day, the people are going to the shops. They see the Giant. He is playing with the children in the most beautiful garden.

All day long the children play. In the evening, they come and say goodbye to the Giant.

'But where's your little friend?' he asks them. The young boy is the Giant's **favourite** because he remembers the child's kiss.

'We don't know,' one of the children answers. 'He isn't here now.'

favourite the one that someone likes best

'Well, he must come again tomorrow. Please tell him that,' the Giant says. 'Where does he live?'

'We're not **sure**,' a different child says. 'We don't know him.'

When the Giant hears this, he is very **sad**.

Every afternoon, when school finishes, the children come and play with the Giant. But the Giant's favourite, the little boy, never comes back. The Giant is very nice to all the children, but he wants to see his first little friend again. He speaks about him a lot. 'I'd like to see him again one day,' he often says.

sure when you feel that something is true

sad not happy

After many years, the Giant is old and **weak**. He cannot play any more. So he sits in a nice big chair, and he watches the children's **games**. He looks at his garden happily, too.

weak not strong

game something that you play; tennis and football are games

'I have many beautiful flowers,' he says. 'But the children are the most beautiful flowers of all.'

READING CHECK

Choose the correct pictures.

a Who sees the Giant playing with the children at twelve o'clock?

1 ☑ people from the town
2 ☐ the Autumn
3 ☐ some flowers

b What does the Giant remember of the boy in the tree?

1 ☐ his eyes
2 ☐ his hair
3 ☐ his kiss

c When do the children visit the Giant's garden?

1 ☐ after breakfast
2 ☐ after work
3 ☐ after school

d What does the Giant watch when he is older?

1 ☐ the television
2 ☐ the children's games
3 ☐ the birds

e What, for the Giant, is the most beautiful thing in his garden?

1 ☐ the birds
2 ☐ the flowers
3 ☐ the children

GUESS WHAT

What happens in the next chapter? Label the sentences G (Giant) or B (boy).

a He looks out of his window at the garden in winter. ....
b He is wearing only white. ....
c He is suddenly angry. ....
d He smiles. ....
e He talks about his garden. ....
f He dies happily. ....

The little boy

The Giant

CHAPTER 6
The wounds of love

One winter morning, when he is getting up, the Giant looks out of his window. The winter doesn't matter to him now. The spring is sleeping at that time of the year, he knows, and the flowers are in their beds under the ground.

Suddenly, he sees something wonderful. 'Can it be true?' he cries.

Far across the garden in one corner, there is a tree with beautiful white blossoms all over it. There are silver apples on its golden branches. And the little boy – his favourite – is standing under the tree. He is all in white.

The Giant runs down to his front door, and out into the garden. He goes quickly across it to the child. But when he comes near, his face is suddenly angry. 'Where do these **wounds** come from?' he cries.

Because there on the boy's hands are the wounds of two **nails**. And the wounds of two nails are on his little feet.

'Who is **guilty** of this? Tell me, and I can take my big **sword** and kill him!'

'No,' the child answers. 'Because these are the wounds of love.'

'Who are you?' the Giant says quietly, and he **kneels** before the child.

wound a hole in the body from a knife or a nail

nail a thick metal pin for fixing one thing to another thing

guilty doing something bad in the past

sword a long knife for fighting

kneel to go on your knees

Then the child smiles at the Giant, and tells him, 'You remember me from before, here in your garden. And today you are coming away with me to my garden – **Paradise**.'

When the children run into the garden that afternoon, they find the Giant under the tree. He is dead now. And there are beautiful white blossoms all over him.

Paradise the happy garden of God, where good people go when they die

READING CHECK

Put these sentences in order. Number them 1–10.

a ☐ The boy asks the Giant to his garden, Paradise.

b ☐ The boy smiles at the Giant.

c ☐ The children find the dead Giant under the blossom tree.

d ☐ The Giant dies.

e ☐ The Giant kneels in front of the boy.

f ☐ The Giant looks out of his window at his garden.

g ☐ The Giant runs out of his house to the little boy.

h ☐ The Giant sees nail wounds on the boy's hands and feet.

i ☐ The Giant sees the little boy under a white blossom tree.

j ☐ The old Giant gets up one winter morning.

GUESS WHAT

What does the Giant do in Paradise after the story finishes? Tick the boxes and add your own ideas.

a ☐ He plays with the children there.

b ☐ He works in the garden.

c ☐ He talks to the little boy about his wounds of love.

d ☐ He meets the little boy's father.

e ☐ He meets a beautiful woman Giant.

f ☐ He meets the Cornish Giant when he arrives.

g ☐ ....

h ☐ ....

i ☐ ....

23

Project A *Personification*

personification is when a writer describes a thing like a person.

1 Match the things with what they do in the story.

a	The Flower	**1**	…moves things here and there all day.
b	The Frost	**2**	…puts her cold, white coat on the ground.
c	The Hail	**3**	…puts its head up out of the ground.
d	The North Wind	**4**	…puts silver on the trees.
e	The Snow	**5**	…hits the Giant's roof noisily.

2 Read the notes in the table about the Autumn. Complete the text on page 25.

Who is she?	Autumn
What does she look like?	golden hair and brown eyes
How old is she?	about 50
What does she wear?	a red and yellow dress
What is in her hands?	lots of fruit and vegetables
What does she do?	visits people's gardens; puts golden apples on trees
Where does she live?	in a big golden tree-house on a dark brown hill
What kind of person is she?	very generous; loves giving things to people

.... has .... hair and .... eyes. She is about .... years old and she wears a .... and ....

In her hands she has lots of .... and ....

She .... people's gardens and puts .... on the trees there.

She lives in a big .... on a dark ....

She is a very .... person. She loves .... to ....

Winter   *Spring*   *Summer*

3 **Choose a different time of year. Imagine it is a person. Complete the table.**

Who is he/she?	
What does he/she look like?	
How old is he/she?	
What does he/she wear?	
What is in his/her hands?	
What does he/she do?	
Where does he/she live?	
What kind of person is he/she?	

4 **Write about your time of year using personification. Use your notes in Activity 3 and the text in Activity 2 to help you.**

Project B *Writing a postcard*

1 Read this postcard. Which part of the story is it about?

Dear Cornish Giant,

Thank you for a wonderful time in Cornwall! I'm back home now. I'm angry because children come after school and play in my garden. I don't like children. So I'm putting a wall around my garden. Now the children must play in the road.

Write soon!

Mr Selfish Giant

Mr Cornish Giant
Cornish Road
Cornwall
CO1 UOK

chapter	
page	
lines	

2 **Write this postcard with punctuation. Use the postcard in Activity 1 to help you.**

dear north wind were having a
wonderful time in the selfish giants
garden its winter here all the year the
frost is putting silver on the trees and i
leave my cold white coat on the ground
every day you must come and stay
with us you can make a lot of noise
and move things here and there all day
come soon mrs snow

Mr North Wind
Windy Street
North Pole
NP2 1CC

....

....

....

....

....

....

....

....

3 **Which part of the story is the postcard in Activity 2 about?**

chapter	
page	
lines	

4 **Write a postcard from the Selfish Giant to the Cornish Giant about a different part of the story. Your classmates must guess which part.**

WORD WORK 1

1 Find words from Chapters 1 and 2 in the flowers to match the pictures.

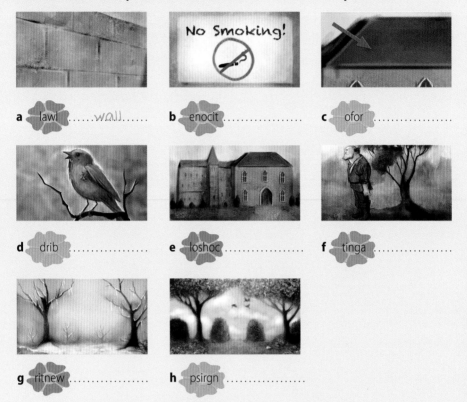

a lawl ......*wall*...... **b** enocit .... **c** ofor ....

d drib .... **e** loshoc .... **f** tinga ....

g ritnew .... **h** psirgn ....

2 Complete the sentences with words from Chapters 1 and 2.

a Look at the .....*frost*..... on the window! It makes beautiful pictures.

b The garden's all white today. There's .... on everything.

c There are lots of trees .... grandmother's house.

d He doesn't help people. He's a very .... man.

e She's old and has got lots of .... in her hair now.

f Listen to that! The .... is very noisy tonight.

g Ouch! My head! That isn't rain. It's ....!

h What's that on the .... near your feet?

WORD WORK 2

1 Look at the pictures. Complete the crossword with words from Chapters 3 and 4.

ACROSS

3

4

5

7

9

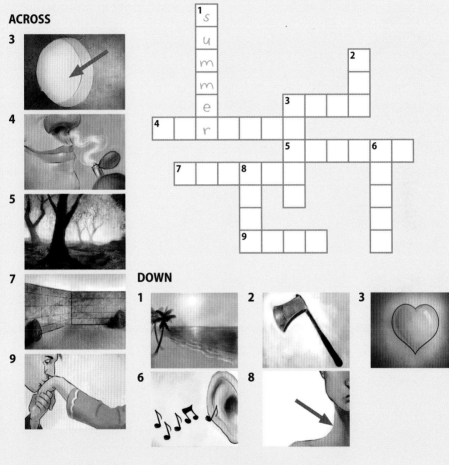

1 S
u
m
m
e
r

DOWN

1

2

3

6

8

2 Complete each sentence with a word or phrase from the box.

    blossom   ~~branches~~   golden   knocking down   other

a There are lots of birds on the …branches… of that tree.

b Look at these apples! They're a nice .... colour.

c Can you see the white .... on all the trees? It's spring!

d Oh, no! They're .... our old school!

e I like this picture, but I don't like the .... pictures in the book.

WORD WORK 3

1 These words don't match the pictures. Correct them.

a ~~sword~~ ......nail...... **b** sad.................. **c** wound..................

d weak.................. **e** nail.................. **f** kneel..................

2 Complete the sentences with words from Chapters 5 and 6.

    a Adam and Eve leave P a r a d i s e after they eat the apple.

    b Which is your _ a _ o u _ i _ e book?

    c Is he the killer? This is the question. Is he _ u i _ _ _?

    d 'Do you want to come tonight?' 'I'm not _ u _ e. Perhaps.'

    e Can we play a _ a _ e of tennis later?

GRAMMAR

GRAMMAR CHECK

Linkers: and, but, so and because

and links two parts of a sentence with the same idea.

There are trees in the Giant's garden and there are flowers, too.

but links two parts of a sentence with different ideas.

The Giant is away in Cornwall, but he comes back home.

so links two parts of a sentence talking about the result of something.

He puts a wall around his garden <u>so the children can't go in</u>.

(result of first part of sentence)

because links two parts of a sentence talking about the reason for something.

The children run away from the Giant <u>because they are afraid</u>.

(reason for first part of sentence)

1 Circle the correct word to complete each sentence.

  a It's spring all over the country, *but* / *so* in the Giant's garden it is winter.

  b The children can't visit the garden *so* / *because* they play in the road.

  c The birds don't sing in the garden *but* / *because* there are no children there.

  d The flower sees the notice *and* / *because* he is sorry for the children.

  e Most people don't like the cold, *so* / *but* the Snow and the Frost love it.

  f The North Wind comes on a visit *because* / *but* the Snow and the Frost ask him.

  g The Hail's suit is the colour of smoke *and* / *but* cold smoke comes from his mouth.

  h The Giant is selfish *so* / *but* the Autumn doesn't bring apples to him.

  i The Hail stops making a noise *and* / *but* the North Wind is quiet.

GRAMMAR CHECK

Present Simple: third person –s

We add –s to the infinitive without *to* to make the third person (*he / she / it*) form of the Present Simple.

The Giant finds the children in his garden.

When verbs end in –o, –ch, –ss, or –sh, we add –es to make the third person form.

finish – They go there when school finishes.

When verbs end in consonant + –y, we change the y to i and add –es.

cry – 'What are you doing here?' he cries.

The verbs *be* and *have* are irregular.

The Giant is very angry. ✔ *The Giant bes very angry.* ✘

He has (got) a big axe. ✔ *He haves a big axe.* ✘

We can use the Present Simple to re-tell a story.

2 Complete these sentences with the verbs in brackets in the Present Simple.

a The Giant ..... *hears* ..... (hear) music at his open window.

b 'The spring's here at last!' he .... (cry).

c He .... (look) out at his garden.

d He .... (see) something in one corner.

e 'Get up, little boy,'................. (say) the tree.

f The Giant .... (watch) all of this from the window of his house.

g His cold heart .... (be) suddenly warmer after this.

h He .... (go) out into the garden.

i The little boy .... (have) his head sadly in his hands.

j The Giant .... (do) something very good and beautiful.

k He .... (put) the little boy up in the branches of the tree.

l The boy .... (kiss) the Giant happily.

GRAMMAR CHECK

Present Continuous: affirmative and negative

We use the Present Continuous to talk about things happening now. We make the Present Continuous affirmative of most verbs with the verb be + the –ing form of the verb.

The Giant is standing next to the tree.

When a verb ends in consonant + –e, we take away the e and add –ing.

smile – The boy is smiling now.

When verbs end in a stressed short vowel + consonant, we double the final consonant and add –ing.

run – The children are running away.

We put n't (not) with the verb be to make the Present Continuous negative.

The children aren't (are not) walking.

3 Complete the text about the picture with the verbs in the correct form.

The little boy a) ...is standing... (stand) in the tree and he b) ....
(look) at the Giant. The Giant c) .... (smile). Some children
d) .... (come) back into the garden through the hole in the wall. They
e) .... (not cry) and they f) .... (not laugh). They
g) .... (watch) the Giant carefully. Some birds h) .... (sit)
in the tree with the boy in it. They i) .... (sing) happily. The tree
j) .... (blossom) and the snow k) .... (go) quickly from
the ground. It l) .... (not rain). It's warm and the sun is in the sky.

Read *Dominoes* for pleasure, or to develop language skills. It's your choice.

Each *Domino* reader includes:
- a good story to enjoy
- integrated activities to develop reading skills and increase vocabulary
- task-based projects – perfect for CEFR portfolios
- contextualized grammar activities

Each *Domino* pack contains a reader, and an excitingly dramatized audio recording of the story

If you liked this *Domino*, read these:

The Little Match Girl
Hans Andersen

It's a cold winter's day, and a poor little girl can't sell any of her matches to people in the street. She can't go home with no money. But how can she stay warm? That 31st December, the little match girl sees rich people's homes, Christmas trees, and wonderful things to eat. She sadly remembers her kind grandmother – now dead and up in heaven. Can the New Year make things any better for the poor young girl?

Ali Baba and the Forty Thieves
retold by Janet Hardy-Gould

After Ali Baba finds a thieves' treasure cave, he is suddenly rich. Then his brother Kasim visits the cave, and things go wrong. The forty thieves find Kasim there, kill him, and cut him into four pieces. What can Ali Baba do? He wants to bury his brother quietly. But how can he? Morgiana, his servant-girl, has the answer. But what can she do when the thieves find Ali Baba and want to kill him, too?

	CEFR	Cambridge Exams	IELTS	TOEFL iBT	TOEIC
Level 3	B1	PET	4.0	57-86	550
Level 2	A2–B1	KET-PET	3.0-4.0	–	390
Level 1	A1–A2	YLE Flyers/KET	3.0	–	225
Starter & Quick Starter	A1	YLE Movers	1.0–2.0	–	–

You can find details and a full list of books and teachers' resources on our website:
www.oup.com/elt/gradedreaders